One DIRECTION

Joanne
Mattern

Mitchell Lane

PUBLISHERS

P.O. Box 196
Hockessin, Delaware 19707
Visit us on the web: www.mitchelllane.com
Comments? Email us: mitchelllane@mitchelllane.com

Mitchell Lane
PUBLISHERS

Printing   1   2   3   4   5   6   7   8   9

Blue Banner Biographies

Adele	Ice Cube	Nancy Pelosi
Alicia Keys	Ja Rule	Natasha Bedingfield
Allen Iverson	Jamie Foxx	One Direction
Ashanti	Jay-Z	Orianthi
Ashlee Simpson	Jennifer Hudson	Orlando Bloom
Ashton Kutcher	Jennifer Lopez	P. Diddy
Avril Lavigne	Jessica Simpson	Peyton Manning
Blake Lively	J. K. Rowling	Pink
Bow Wow	Joe Flacco	Prince William
Brett Favre	John Legend	Queen Latifah
Britney Spears	Justin Berfield	Rihanna
Bruno Mars	Justin Timberlake	Robert Downey Jr.
CC Sabathia	Kanye West	Robert Pattinson
Carrie Underwood	Kate Hudson	Ron Howard
Chris Brown	Katy Perry	Sean Kingston
Chris Daughtry	Keith Urban	Selena
Christina Aguilera	Kelly Clarkson	Shakira
Ciara	Kenny Chesney	Shia LaBeouf
Clay Aiken	Ke$ha	Shontelle Layne
Cole Hamels	Kristen Stewart	Soulja Boy Tell 'Em
Condoleezza Rice	Lady Gaga	Stephenie Meyer
Corbin Bleu	Lance Armstrong	Taylor Swift
Daniel Radcliffe	Leona Lewis	T.I.
David Ortiz	Lil Wayne	Timbaland
David Wright	Lindsay Lohan	Tim McGraw
Derek Jeter	Ludacris	Tim Tebow
Drew Brees	Mariah Carey	Toby Keith
Eminem	Mario	Usher
Eve	Mary J. Blige	Vanessa Anne Hudgens
Fergie	Mary-Kate and Ashley Olsen	Will.i.am
Flo Rida	Megan Fox	Zac Efron
Gwen Stefani	Miguel Tejada	

Library of Congress Cataloging-in-Publication Data
Mattern, Joanne, 1963–
  One direction / by Joanne Mattern.
     p. cm. — (Blue banner biographies)
Includes bibliographical references and index.
ISBN 978-1-61228-407-1 (library bound)
1. One Direction (Musical group)—Juvenile literature. 2. Rock musicians—England—Biography—Juvenile literature. I. Title.
 ML3930.O66M37 2013
 782.42164092'2—dc23
 [B]
                                                                                                    2012026539
eBook ISBN: 9781612284088

ABOUT THE AUTHOR: Joanne Mattern first learned about One Direction thanks to her daughter Leanne, who is a loyal Directioner. Leanne encouraged her mother to write this book and assisted her with the research. Joanne has written many celebrity biographies for Mitchell Lane, including books about Jennifer Hudson, the Jonas Brothers, Michelle Obama, LeBron James, and Blake Lively. She lives in New York State with her husband, four children, and an assortment of pets.

PUBLISHER'S NOTE: The following story has been thoroughly researched, and to the best of our knowledge represents a true story. While every possible effort has been made to ensure accuracy, the publisher will not assume liability for damages caused by inaccuracies in the data and makes no warranty on the accuracy of the information contained herein. This story has not been authorized or endorsed by One Direction.

Blue Banner Biography

Zayn Malik

Niall Horan

Liam Payne

Louis
Tomlinson

Harry
Styles

One Direction shows off their silly side at a party celebrating the release of their first single, "What Makes You Beautiful."

A Second Chance

A line of contestants stood on the stage of the British television show *The X Factor,* all waiting to hear their fates. Among the contestants were Harry Styles, Liam Payne, Louis Tomlinson, Niall Horan, and Zayn Malik. Each one hoped to win the competition and be named Britain's newest music star.

The boys and the other contestants had just finished a difficult part of the show known as Bootcamp. Now, all the singers in the "Boys" category were lined up on the stage, waiting to hear who had made it through to the next level of the competition . . . and who would be going home.

Finally, after seemingly endless moments of suspense, the judges announced the news. For Harry, Liam, Louis, Niall, and Zayn, the news was bad. They had all been eliminated from the show. It looked like their journeys to stardom were over.

The boys went backstage. They were very upset, and several of them were even crying. They all believed that their dreams were finished.

But this would not be the end of the road for the young singers. The judges were talking about them, and they had made an important decision. Judge Nicole Scherzinger had seen something special in the five boys, and she came up with an idea. She suggested to the other judges that the five boys become a band and compete in *The X Factor*'s "Groups" category. The other judges, Simon Cowell and Louis Walsh, agreed. As Cowell later explained to *Rolling Stone*, "We had high hopes for two or three of them in particular, and then it all kind of fell apart at one of the latter stages. Interestingly, when they left, I had a bad feeling that maybe we shouldn't have lost them and maybe there was something else we should do with them. And this is when the idea came about that we should see if they could work as a group."

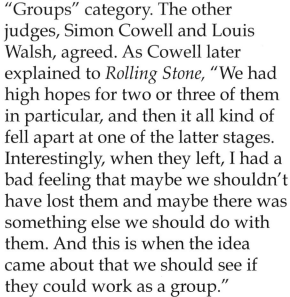

The boys decided that there was no way they were going to say no to this second chance.

The five young men were called back onstage and stood before the judges once again. "The minute they stood there for the first time together—it was a weird feeling," Cowell said to *Rolling Stone*. "They just looked like a group at that point." The judges gave the boys a choice. They could join together and continue to compete as a group, or they could go home. The boys were given five minutes to decide what they wanted to do.

At first, some of the boys thought the idea was a little strange. Liam explained that they had gotten along well at Bootcamp, but they thought of each other as competition at the time. Suddenly, they were being asked to work together

The members of One Direction pose with Simon Cowell, their mentor and judge on The X Factor, *before the show's finale in December 2010. Although the band did not win the competition, they went on to achieve even greater success thanks to Cowell's support.*

as a team. As Liam told the *South Wales Echo*, "My first thought was, 'are we going to make this work when we don't know each other?' It was such a leap of faith."

The boys decided that there was no way they were going to say no to this second chance. They went back onstage and told the judges that they were willing to team up and become a band. All five were excited, but they had a long road ahead of them. They barely knew each other, and had never performed together. All of them wondered if they could make this new opportunity work.

Before 1D

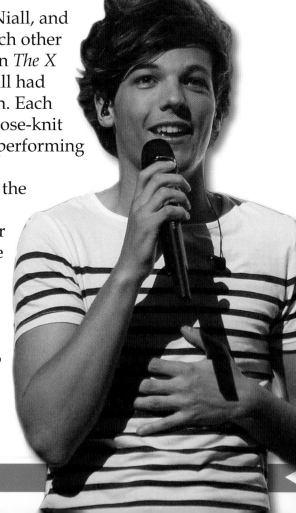

Harry, Liam, Louis, Niall, and Zayn had never met each other before they appeared on *The X Factor*. However, they all had some things in common. Each one had come from a close-knit family and had begun performing at an early age.

Louis Tomlinson is the oldest member of One Direction, or 1D as their fans often call them. He was born on December 24, 1991, in a town in northern England called Doncaster. Louis's parents split up when he was young and he was raised by his mother and stepfather. He thinks of his stepfather as his father, and shares his last name with him as well. Louis got his first taste of show business through his sisters, twins Daisy and Phoebe. When they were babies, the girls appeared on a television show called *Fat Friends.* Louis sometimes worked as an extra on the show. He enjoyed acting so much that he attended an acting school for a few years and earned small parts on several British television shows.

Although Louis was a good actor, he wasn't a very good student. He even had to repeat a year of high school because he spent too much time going to parties. In the band's biography, *Dare to Dream: Life as One Direction,* Louis admitted that he failed "mainly because I'd been too busy having fun . . . I was out all the time in that first year." Louis finally settled down and took school more seriously. He also worked on singing and performing by appearing in school plays.

Zayn Malik was born on January 12, 1993, in Bradford, England. His grandfather on his father's side is from Pakistan, and his mother is English and Irish. Because of his mixed ethnic heritage, Zayn had trouble fitting in at school. But when he was twelve years old, he switched to a different school that had a more diverse student body and he felt much more comfortable there.

While other members of the band grew up listening to pop and rock, Zayn was listening to R&B and hip-hop. Like Louis, Zayn appeared in several school plays. "I absolutely loved being on stage and becoming somebody else," he wrote in *Dare to Dream.* "Back then it was all about being on stage playing a character."

Liam Payne was born on August 29, 1993, in Wolverhampton in western England. Liam faced many serious health problems when he was young. He was three weeks premature and unresponsive when he was born. When he was four years old, doctors discovered that one of Liam's kidneys was not working. But as he got older, his health improved and he joined his school's cross-country running and basketball teams.

When Liam was twelve years old, some older boys bullied him because of the clothes he wore. "I needed to find a way to defend myself," Liam wrote in *Dare to Dream.* He joined a local gym where he took up boxing. "It gave me so much confidence. It was nerve-wracking at first, but I got pretty good over the next couple of years." Liam eventually found the courage to stand up to the bullies. He later told fans in a video interview with *The New Zealand Herald*, "You have to tell someone. You have to stand up to it . . . You make sure something's done about it, and it will slowly stop."

Niall Horan is the only member of One Direction who was not born in England. He was born on September 13, 1993, in Mullingar, Ireland. Niall's parents divorced when he was young and he spent a few years moving back and forth between their homes. When he was a little older, he moved into his father's house so he could be closer to school and his friends.

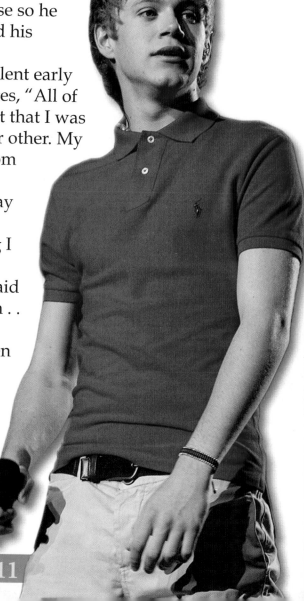

Niall showed musical talent early on. In *Dare to Dream*, he writes, "All of my family remember the fact that I was always singing something or other. My auntie used to come over from America every summer and we'd go on holiday to Galway in the west of Ireland. Once when we were driving along I was singing Garth Brooks in the back of the car and she said she thought the radio was on . . . My auntie said she always knew I'd be famous from then on." Later, Niall played the guitar and sang in several local talent shows.

Harry Styles is the youngest member of One Direction, born on February 1, 1994, in

Holmes Chapel, England. When he was seven years old, Harry's parents divorced, and Harry later wrote in *Dare to Dream*, "that was quite a weird time. I remember crying about it." Harry's mother later remarried, and Harry now has close relationships with both of his parents and his stepfather.

Harry always enjoyed singing. His father was a fan of legendary music star Elvis Presley and played his records for Harry when he was a little boy. Harry first performed in public when he was in his early teens. Some friends were putting together a band called White Eskimo and asked Harry to join. The group entered the school's Battle of the Bands competition, and they won. At that point, the band began to take their music more seriously, practicing regularly, and performing at a wedding and other events. Harry had no idea that one day he and four other young men would be competing in a much bigger competition.

CHAPTER 3

The X Factor Challenge

*L*ike millions of other people in the United Kingdom, Harry, Liam, Louis, Niall, and Zayn were big fans of *The X Factor*. The television show first aired in 2004 as a contest to find a new singing star and award that person or group with a £1 million recording contract. There are four categories of performers on the show: Boys, Girls, Over 25s, and Groups. If performers can make it through two sets of auditions before producers and a panel of judges, they move on to a challenge called Bootcamp. In Bootcamp, they work on perfecting their singing and dancing skills before facing an elimination round.

The remaining contestants then travel to the judges' houses, where they continue to perform. At the houses, they are told whether they will be competing on live television and which judge will be their mentor. Each week, the finalists perform, and the television audience votes. The contestant who receives the lowest number of votes is sent home. Until 2011, the judging panel was led by Simon Cowell, a music executive who is best known to American audiences as a former judge on the U.S. hit show *American*

Idol. Cowell is still the executive producer of *The X Factor,* which became the biggest television talent competition in Europe. A U.S. version was launched in 2011.

By the time they were in their mid-teens, all of the future One Direction members had discovered a love for singing and performing. Auditioning for *The X Factor* seemed like the chance of a lifetime for the five boys. As Harry told *People* magazine, "I got such a thrill out of singing in front of people. I realized I wanted to do it more and more."

Like millions of other people in the United Kingdom, Harry, Liam, Louis, Niall, and Zayn were big fans of The X Factor.

Although Harry dreamed of being on *The X Factor,* he didn't have enough nerve to actually apply. It was his mother who filled out the application and sent it in. Zayn was also nervous; he admits that he thought about sending in the application for two years before he finally found the courage to do it.

Niall had wanted to try out for *The X Factor* for a long time, and Louis had auditioned for the show in 2009, but didn't make it past the first round. Liam had also tried out for *The X Factor* before. He auditioned in 2008, when he was just fourteen years old. He advanced as far as the Judges' Houses in the competition, when he was sent home. The rejection hurt, but Liam later realized that the timing wasn't right for him. "I felt quite grown-up at the time and like I was capable of handling everything that came with being on the show. But looking back now at all we've been through, there is no way I could have handled it," he wrote in *Dare to Dream*. "If I had made the live shows I wouldn't have known what had hit me."

In 2010, all five boys auditioned and made it into Bootcamp, but were eliminated. When the judges asked them to return to the show as a group, the boys wanted to make the most of the opportunity. But there were many challenges ahead for the new group.

Harry, Louis, Liam, Niall, and Zayn had just five weeks to put their band together and come up with a performance that was good enough to impress the judges. Harry's stepfather owned a small house in Cheshire, England, and he told Harry that he and his new group members could stay there and rehearse.

They spent some time working on their music, but mostly the boys spent the first few days in the house getting

One Direction arrives at Fountain Studios in London for X Factor rehearsals. In addition to singing, Niall (far right) often plays guitar onstage.

to know each other. They played soccer and stayed up late talking and joking around. It didn't take long for the five singers to become friends. They also decided on a name for their group. Harry suggested "One Direction" and everyone agreed. It was appropriate, since now they were all going in the same direction as a group.

Harry, Louis, Liam, Niall, and Zayn had just five weeks to put their band together and come up with a performance.

After a week, it was time to get down to making music. "The first few days were quite tough," Liam told the *South Wales Echo.* "We all had different ideas, but we didn't really know what a group was about." The fact that the boys didn't have much formal musical training didn't help either. "We didn't know what a harmony was," Zayn said. "We all just sang in unison for two weeks."

Finally, it was time to go back to *The X Factor.* They traveled to Simon Cowell's house in Marbella, Spain, for their first performance together as a group. When they had finished singing, the boys couldn't tell from Cowell's reaction whether they'd impressed him or not. Cowell told *Rolling Stone* he realized how good they were "after about a millionth of a second. I tried to keep a straight face for a bit of drama for the show . . . The second they left I jumped out of my chair and said, 'These guys are incredible!' They just had it. They had this confidence. They were fun. They worked out the arrangements themselves. They were like a gang of friends, and kind of fearless as well."

One Direction performs during The X Factor Live *tour in 2011. The boys share the spotlight when they perform, taking turns singing solos onstage.*

One Direction quickly became a fan favorite on the show. *The X Factor* broadcast behind-the-scenes videos of the boys joking around and being silly, and their fans loved them even more. For ten weeks, it looked like they could go all the way to the top. Expectations were high for the group going into the finale.

Halfway through the final show, it was time to narrow the competition from three acts to two. When it was finally announced that One Direction had been eliminated, the boys were disappointed, and their fans were shocked.

Although they were upset, once again, One Direction's journey was not over. Simon Cowell met with the band and told them he had arranged a recording contract for them. One Direction was about to get even bigger.

CHAPTER 4

Fan Power!

One Direction signed with Syco Records, a British label that is owned by Simon Cowell and Sony Music Entertainment. But before the band could start recording, they joined nine other *X Factor* acts for a tour of Great Britain that lasted from February until April 2011. The musicians performed for more than 500,000 people throughout the United Kingdom, which includes England, Northern Ireland, Scotland, and Wales.

The band loved performing in front of huge crowds and found the experience thrilling. "The rush you get being on stage in front of so many people is indescribable. I wish everyone could have that feeling . . . I loved the tour so much I never wanted it to stop," Harry wrote in *Dare to Dream*. Harry and his bandmates also enjoyed meeting their fans. "It really doesn't get much better than that," Harry wrote, recalling the group's performance in front of a crowd of screaming fans on the first night of the tour.

The boys also wrote a best-selling book about their *X Factor* experiences, called *Forever Young*. When it was time to go into the studio to work on their first album, Simon

Cowell brought in top songwriters to work with them, including *American Idol* winner Kelly Clarkson. The band was thrilled to travel to Los Angeles to record the album, since most of them had never been outside of Europe before.

In November 2011, One Direction's album, *Up All Night,* was released in Great Britain. It became the fastest-selling debut album in Britain that year and produced three top ten songs on the UK Singles Chart: "What Makes You Beautiful," "Gotta Be You," and "One Thing."

Meanwhile, word about One Direction was spreading to the United States. Usually, bands become well-known because their record companies and management spend a lot of money on publicity. They advertise the band's records on the radio and in magazines, and band members give interviews and appear on television shows to get the word out. Things happened very differently with One Direction. This band became famous in America largely through social media sites like Facebook, Twitter, and YouTube. As Sonny Takhar, the managing director of Syco Records, explained to *The Guardian,* "social media has become the new radio, it's never broken an act globally like this before." Will Bloomfield, the manager of One Direction, agrees, telling *Rolling Stone* that "these guys live online, and so do their fans."

One Direction fans call themselves "Directioners." They wrote about the band on Facebook and Twitter and encouraged their friends and followers to watch YouTube videos of the band's performances. It was the fans' dedication and social media presence that really made One

Direction popular with teenagers in the United States at a time when most adults in the U.S. had never heard of them. "It's played a massive part," Harry told the *Associated Press*. "Twitter, Facebook, and YouTube have been a large percentage of the reason we've been known outside of the UK . . . We owe a massive thank you to the fans." Bandmate Louis agrees, adding, "whenever you ask anyone how they know about us, it's always Twitter or Tumblr or something like that."

The band was thrilled to travel to Los Angeles to record the album, since most of them had never been outside of Europe before.

By early 2012, One Direction was already a sensation in the United States. When *Up All Night* was finally released in the United States and Canada in March 2012, it went straight to Number One on the Billboard 200. It was the first time in history that a British group's first album debuted on the U.S. charts at Number One. The single, "What Makes You Beautiful," was released in February 2012 and shot to Number Four on the Billboard Hot 100 chart. As of June 2012, *Up All Night* had sold more than 2.3 million copies around the world.

To promote the album's U.S. release, the band came to New York City and made several appearances. On March 12, they were scheduled to perform in *The Today Show*'s studio. However, so many fans showed up that the concert had to be moved outdoors to Rockefeller Plaza. About 15,000 fans crowded the streets to see their idols. After the show, *Today* producer Melissa Lonner told *Billboard*, "One Direction is relatively unknown with no hits yet. They basically exploded, and all the adults

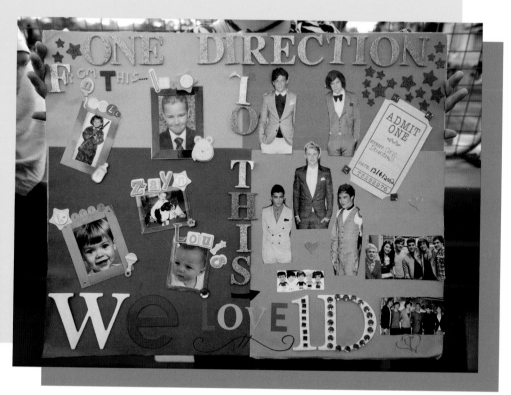

This collage was made by One Direction fans in Australia. One Direction is very grateful for their fans' support and dedication. They love when Directioners display posters and T-shirts during their concerts.

are saying, 'Who are these people, and how do they know about it?'"

One Direction then set out on a short tour of the United States, Australia, and New Zealand. Between April and July, they scheduled twenty-eight shows, all of which quickly sold out. *Up All Night: The Live Tour* is a DVD recording of a show from their winter tour of Great Britain. The DVD debuted at Number One on the Billboard DVD chart, selling 76,000 copies in the first week of release. One Direction's DVD sold more copies than the Number One album in the country that week—something which had never happened before in chart history. Their devoted Directioners just could not get enough.

CHAPTER 5

Looking Ahead

*I*n June 2012, Nick Gatfield, the chairman of Sony Music UK, announced that One Direction was already a $50 million business and he expected that figure to double to $100 million over the next year. In addition to record and ticket sales, One Direction's business side includes product sales and advertising agreements with Pokemon, Nokia, HarperCollins, and Hasbro. The band also earns money from clothes, posters, jewelry, and other products featuring their pictures and stories.

The group has many plans for the future. In May 2012, they began recording their second album. Although they continue to use outside songwriters, the band members plan to write some songs as well. Harry Styles told *The Sun,* "We're always writing on the road and in hotels and airports. We don't ever want our music to sound like a 40-year-old man in an office has written it and given it to us to perform." The album is scheduled for release near the end of 2012.

In 2013, One Direction will go back on the road for another world tour. The tour includes more than 100 shows

In 2012, One Direction went on tour in the United States, where tickets sold out almost immediately. Here the band performs at the Beacon Theatre in New York City on May 26, 2012.

in the United Kingdom, North America, Australia, and New Zealand. The tour sold out within days of being announced, and the band even added extra shows to the schedule.

One Direction has been credited with bringing back the "boy band," especially in the United States. In the 1990s, boy bands such as *NSYNC, the Backstreet Boys, and New Kids on the Block dominated pop radio in the United States. As the new millennium began, however, solo hip-hop artists ruled the air waves. Many people believe that One Direction is changing that trend. The group has been part of a so-called "British invasion" of artists and bands from Great Britain that have become very popular in the United States, like Jessie J and The Wanted.

The members of One Direction are comfortable with their "boy band" image, but want fans to know that they aren't cardboard cutouts without their own ideas. Simon Cowell agrees. "They had good taste and they understood the kind of group they wanted to be. They didn't want to be molded. I'm not interested in working with people like that either," Cowell told *Rolling Stone*.

One Direction's members also love to give back to people who need help. Along with other *X Factor* finalists,

One Direction is dedicated to giving back to their fans and to people in need. The boys pose backstage during a BBC Children in Need charity event in London in November 2011.

Niall, Zayn, Liam, Louis, and Harry walk through the streets of London on their way to attend Heart Radio's annual Have a Heart Fundraising Appeal to aid children's charities in England.

the band recorded a cover of David Bowie's classic song, "Heroes," to raise money for Help for Heroes, a charity that provides medical care and support for injured British soldiers. One Direction's members also contributed to a celebrity cookbook, called *A Dish For A Wish*, to raise money for Rays of Sunshine Children's Charity. This charity grants the wishes of sick children in the United Kingdom. The band worked with Rays of Sunshine to grant some wishes themselves by spending time with two ill teenage girls. One Direction has also auctioned off tickets to raise money for London's Great Ormond Street Hospital's Children's Charity and the American Red Cross.

What will the future hold for One Direction? All the band members have big dreams. In *Dare to Dream*, Harry wrote, "We want to have number ones, travel a lot, go back to America, and have as much fun as possible." Most of all, Harry, Liam, Louis, Zayn, and Niall want to keep making their fans happy for years to come.

In 2012, One Direction won their first BRIT Award, which is a prestigious award in Great Britain, similar to the Grammy Awards in the United States. The band beat out popular UK singer Adele to win the award for Best Single for their song, "What Makes You Beautiful."

1991   Louis Tomlinson born on December 24.

1993   Zayn Malik born on January 12; Liam Payne born on August 29; Niall Horan born on September 13.

1994   Harry Styles born on February 1.

2006   Zayn acts in a school production of *Grease.*

2008   Liam auditions for *The X Factor,* but is eliminated at the Judges' Houses.

2009   Louis auditions for *The X Factor,* but doesn't advance past the first round; Harry and his band White Eskimo win their school's Battle of the Bands competition.

2010   Niall performs with Lloyd Daniels in Dublin; Louis, Zayn, Liam, Niall, and Harry appear individually on *The X Factor*; they are eliminated but asked to return as a group. The boys form One Direction, placing third in the competition.

2011   One Direction releases its first album, *Up All Night,* which becomes the fastest-selling debut album in the United Kingdom that year.

2012   One Direction makes chart history when *Up All Night* debuts at Number One on the U.S. Billboard 200 chart; the group wins a BRIT Award for Best British Single; recording begins on One Direction's second album.

2013   One Direction tours the United States, the United Kingdom, Australia, and New Zealand.

DISCOGRAPHY

2011   *Up All Night*

APPEARANCES

TELEVISION AND VIDEO

2010   *The X Factor*
2011   *ITV2 Special: One Direction: A Year in the Making*
2012   *Dancing on Ice*
       The Today Show
       Saturday Night Live
       iCarly
       Up All Night: The Live Tour (DVD)

Huntington City
Township Public Library
255 West Park Drive
Huntington, IN 46750

FURTHER READING

Books

Boone, Mary. *One Direction: What Makes You Beautiful.* Chicago: Triumph Books, 2012.

Oliver, Sarah. *One Direction A-Z.* London: John Blake Publishing, 2011.

One Direction. *Dare to Dream: Life as One Direction.* New York: HarperCollins, 2012.

One Direction. *Forever Young: Our Official X Factor Story.* New York: HarperCollins, 2011.

Works Consulted

Corner, Lewis. "One Direction: 'Next Album Will Have More Guitars and Be Grungier.' " *Digital Spy,* February 20, 2012. http://www.digitalspy.co.uk/music/news/a366746/one-direction-next-album-will-have-more-guitars-and-be-grungier.html

Greene, Andy. "Exclusive Q&A: Simon Cowell on One Direction's Rise to Stardom." *Rolling Stone,* April 9, 2012. http://www.rollingstone.com/music/news/exclusive-q-a-simon-cowell-on-one-directions-rise-to-stardom-20120409

Greene, Andy. "The New British Invasion: Boy Bands." *Rolling Stone India,* May 8, 2012. http://rollingstoneindia.com/features/the-new-british-invasion-boy-bands/

Horowitz, Steven J. "One Direction & The Wanted: The Billboard Cover Story." *Billboard,* March 27, 2012. http://www.billboard.com/features/one-direction-the-wanted-the-billboard-cover-1006560552.story

The Hot Hits Live From LA. "One Direction Biography." http://www.thehothits.com/artists/6069/one-direction/bio

"One Direction: Chart Stars in Their Own Words." *The Sun,* September 16, 2011. http://www.thesun.co.uk/sol/homepage/showbiz/bizarre/3817326/One-Direction-Chart-stars-in-their-own-words.html

One Direction. *Dare to Dream: Life as One Direction.* New York: HarperCollins, 2012.

"One Direction Makes US Chart History Again." *Sony Music Entertainment,* June 6, 2012. http://plus.google.com/u/0/116531126913606359895/posts/A5yuZsbeu8M

"One Direction." *People* Collector's Special. June 2012.

"One Direction Prepare for Cardiff Sell-Out Shows." *South Wales Echo,* January 13, 2012. http://www.walesonline.co.uk/showbiz-and-lifestyle/showbiz/2012/01/13/one-direction-prepare-for-cardiff-sell-out-shows-91466-30112196/2/

"One Direction Talk About Bullying." *The New Zealand Herald,* May 7, 2012. http://www.nzherald.co.nz/nz/news/video.cfm?c_id=1&gal_cid=1&gallery_id=125440

"One Direction To Perform On The Today Show In US." 95-106 Capital FM, February 16, 2012. http://www.capitalfm.com/artists/one-direction/news/the-today-show-perform-us/

Pakinkis, Tom. "One Direction Will Become $100M Business Empire, Says Sony." *Music Week,* June 13, 2012. http://www.musicweek.com/story.asp?sectioncode=1&storycode=1049914

Smart, Gordon, ed. "One Direction: Cowell Pays Us Jelly Beans." *The Sun,* April 24, 2012. http://www.thesun.co.uk/sol/homepage/showbiz/bizarre/4275254/One-Direction-moan-about-their-salary-despite-getting-2million-in-bonuses-from-Simon-Cowell.html

Smith, Caspar Llewellyn. "One Direction: The Fab Five Take America." *The Guardian,* March 15, 2012. http://www.guardian.co.uk/music/2012/mar/15/one-direction-fab-five-america

On the Internet

The Official *X Factor* Site
http://xfactor.itv.com

One Direction Website
http://www.onedirectionmusic.com/us/home/

YouTube: One Direction
http://www.youtube.com/user/onedirectionchannel